forgive

LIVING FREE FROM
THE PAIN OF OFFENSE

HAMP LEE III

(com)mission TM
PUBLISHING

MONTGOMERY, ALABAMA

Forgive: Living Free from the Pain of Offense / Hamp Lee III.   2nd ed.

ISBN: 978-1-940042-49-7

CONTENTS

CONTENTS

INTRODUCTION

Sadly, many people experience the sting of offense.[1] Like pricking your finger on a thorny rose bush, the pain is sharp and throbbing. But as the pain from thorns subsides, the pain from offense lingers on —and sometimes becomes worse. The pain we experience often changes how we see and interact with the world around us.

When we look in the mirror, we might not recognize the person back looking at us. We reflect anger, hurt, and rage. We speak through isolation and distrust. We become mere shadows of our former selves just to cope with our pain, sadness, and anger.

When we think of our offense, we sometimes think about what could have been. We think about the innocence and joy we lost and the people who hurt us. And though we remain connected to the day of the offense, we want to be free from it. We want to leave the prison of our pain. We want to see beyond the horizon of offense to experience a life of great possibilities—a place of peace and serenity—a place that allows us to enjoy love and joy everlasting.

---

[1] An offense is defined as a displeasure, annoyance, or resentment brought about by an actual or perceived insult, violation, or disregard for someone's standards, principles, or being.

I wrote *Forgive: Living Free from the Pain of Offense* to help us find healing, love, and forgiveness. I say *us* because I know about the sting of offense firsthand. I know what it is like to be filled with rage. I know what it is like to be happy one second, sad the next, and mad after that. And I know about the desire to be free and whole again.

As I share my journey toward forgiveness, I pray the Lord will help you along your journey. I believe you can experience healing, love, and forgiveness, but you must first address the dark places of your mind, heart, and soul to get there. You must face the offense and pain that stares at you through your mirror. Though the process toward forgiveness might not seem easy, it is one you will never regret taking.

I pray you will allow *Forgive: Living Free from the Pain of Offense* to help you along your journey. May this book help you to find your place of healing, love, and forgiveness.

BEFORE YOU BEGIN

Unpacking the box of offense and unforgiveness is not like a present you receive at Christmas. Instead of discovering things that bring joy and happiness, offense and unforgiveness can uncover some of the most painful feelings, thoughts, and emotions you have ever experienced in your life. They can feel so strong and powerful that they consume your very being—suffocating every ounce of peace, joy, and happiness you thought you had.

Offense and unforgiveness had affected every relationship in my life. I felt like a prisoner in my own mind and skin, unable to breathe or soar beyond its sting and pain. I needed the courage to open my *box*, to face those things that kept me bound and trapped, and work toward healing, love, and forgiveness.

As David once wrote, "*...weeping may endure for a night, but joy cometh in the morning.*"[2] You and I have wept for far too many nights over the offense committed against us. If you endure (Lord willing) for a short while longer, you can experience the joy that comes in the morning. This joy welcomes the sun as it breaks from the horizon, warming your soul, and

---

[2] Psalm 30:5.

lighting a new path to walk upon. But you must first press through the darkness of the night to get to this new day...and it is more than possible with the help of three sources of support:

1. God. You were uniquely created by God for His glory.[3] In Him exists all of our present and future hope.[4] God cares for you and wants to help you.[5] He loves you and has not forgotten you.[6] Please do not give up. Seek Him in prayer, His word, and through praise and worship. Remain committed to your process of healing, love, and forgiveness. You are worth the investment!

2. Friends. Friends can stick closer than a brother or sister, sharpen you when you are feeling weak and dull, and walk with you through tough times.[7] A true friend is someone you can share personal thoughts and sins without him or her thinking something's wrong with you, judging you, or getting overly emotional where he or she cannot provide sound help or counsel.[8] You can simply be yourself. Such a friend is with you in the best and worst of times.

---

[3] Isaiah 43:7, 21.

[4] Psalm 46:1–3, 62:7–8; Acts 17:24–28.

[5] Isaiah 43:1–2, 13.

[6] Psalm 37:25; Hebrews 13:5.

[7] Proverbs 17:17, 18:24, 27:17; Ecclesiastes 4:8–12.

[8] Galatians 6:1–2.

3.   Professional counselors and resources. Like friends, professional counselors and resources such as support websites, hotlines, and call centers can also guide you along your path toward healing, love, and forgiveness. They can share perspectives, options, and other solutions that encourage you, strengthen your resolve, and help you persevere until morning's light.

ORIGINS

Your story of offense and unforgiveness might have begun with a single moment, one act that changed your life ever since. Their offense deeply wounded your heart, mind, and soul. And as time went on, the wound never healed. It exists as a painful and lasting reminder of what happened to you.

As you begin your journey toward healing, love, and forgiveness, it will be essential to return to the origin of the offense. If you are unable or unwilling to address not only the event but your feelings and thoughts, you might not be able to discover the healing, love, and forgiveness you need.

Like a GPS, the origin of your offense is your starting point toward your final destination of healing, love, and forgiveness. Before you have a moment to address your origin, I would like to point out two reasons why offense exists in the world today.

Sin

Behold, I was shapen in iniquity; and in sin did my mother conceive me.

—PSALM 51:5

Offense exists in the world because of sin.[9] Its stain rests on every soul in the world, excluding Jesus. And through sin, the world is exposed to many instances of pain, injustice, and hate. You do not have to look any further than your local news to see the impact of sin. Often the offense you and many others experience is because of heinous (sometimes generational) acts committed against your offender—hurting people hurt people—or due to fear, hate, jealousy, anger, pride, etc.

Many people spend most of their adult lives dealing with the pain they experienced in the first eighteen years of their lives. Where they were expecting to be protected, loved, and cared for, they experienced events and circumstances that scarred them well into adulthood—impacting how they parent, relate to others, and live every day. The little child that might have been hurt so many years earlier still cries for help on the inside.

Evil Spirits

For we wrestle not against flesh and blood, but against principalities, against powers, against the rulers of the darkness of this world, against spiritual wickedness in high places.

—EPHESIANS 6:12

---

9 Romans 5:12.

Evil spirits can influence, oppress, and possess people.[10] These spirits seek to disrupt the will of God in your life, as well as those around you. They want to keep you disobedient to God, bound in sin, and eternally separated from Him.[11] But when offense and other hard times come along, we often do not consider this spiritual reality. We want to take out our frustration and anger on our offender, not realizing he or she might have been influenced by spiritual wickedness in high places.

Father, Forgive Them

Then said Jesus, Father, forgive them; for they know not what they do. And they parted his raiment, and cast lots.

—LUKE 23:34

By the time Jesus said this, He had been betrayed, mocked, beaten, falsely accused, flogged, and crucified.[12] But Jesus said, *'Father, forgive them...'*

Jesus understood who was behind His crucifixion. Satan operated through Judas to betray Him.[13] The people who were also acting against Jesus did not

---

[10] 1 Samuel 16:14–15; 1 Kings 22:19–23; Matthew 8:28–34; Mark 1:21–28; Luke 8:26–33; Acts 16:16-18.

[11] Matthew 5:21–26, 6:14–15.

[12] Luke 22:1–23:34.

[13] Luke 22:3; John 14:30.

know they were crucifying the Lord of glory.[14] And Satan did not know Jesus' death was a part of God's plan for the salvation of the world.

Your Origin of Offense

As stated previously, identifying your source of offense is an important first step. It helps you clarify the events and emotions that brought you to where you are today. Now, such an undertaking can open old wounds and scars. Please remember to seek the Lord and use your support system.

Before you continue, please go to the Lord in prayer. Ask for His help to uncover every area of offense and unforgiveness in your life, as well as the contents of your heart, anyone you might have offended, and how you can find healing, love, and forgiveness:

Heavenly Father, I thank you for your compassion that never fails. I ask that you would show me the source of my unforgiveness. Reveal every person I have not forgiven, and the lives I affected because of my unforgiveness. Expose my emotions. Heal my broken heart. Bind up my wounds. Teach me how I can forgive every person who wronged me. Help me see life anew. In the name of Jesus Christ, I pray, Amen.

---

[14] I Corinthians 2:6–8.

Please consider the following questions for each offense you have not forgiven. Begin with the first instance and move forward.

Who have you been unable to forgive?

Describe the circumstances surrounding the offense he or she committed against you.

What emotions have you felt toward him or her?

What actions (if any) have you taken to address your unforgiveness? Were these actions successful? Please explain.

Why do you want to seek forgiveness?

My Story of Offense

My story of offense began in 1999. I was in a relationship where the two of us offended one another in different ways. I forgave the person and asked for forgiveness. Thought I sought to live in love and forgiveness, I did not realize the other person did not forgive me. For the next 17 years, this individual intentionally acted against me. This person took things from me that I might never replace in my lifetime. When God revealed what they had done to me, I was devastated. I was speechless. The pain I had felt like it reached a molecular level in my heart. I was filled with an unspeakable rage for what this person did to me for so many years.

CYCLE OF OFFENSE

One of my favorite childhood games was Tag. Tag was a simple game. Either you were *it*, or you were not. The goal was not to be *it*, but if you were, you would chase the other kids until you tagged someone.

When you choose not to forgive, you slowly transition from the offended to the offender. You become *it*. Whether you realize it or not, you begin to negatively affect everything and everyone around you. This includes those closest to you.

I came to the house one evening when my daughter was washing clothes. She took our towels from the dryer and placed them on the couch without folding them. I went O-F-F. I confronted her about it and started yelling and screaming. I even brought up stuff that had nothing to do with the towels. I treated a small issue as a major problem.

When I stopped yelling and went into my room, I knew why I was so upset. I allowed the offense committed against me to fuel my anger. I became the offender. I was *it*. I took out my frustrations on my daughter. She was an innocent bystander that was now hurt because of my inability to appropriately address my pain.

A little while later, I returned to her room, and I apologized. But through my careless actions, she now was forced to carry a burden she was not meant to. I could not take back my words. I could not ask for a refund. She paid the price for my behavior.

She did not deserve to face such a decision on whether she would forgive me or not. She should be focused on her college studies and enjoying her years as a young adult. I am her daddy. I am supposed to be her protector and guide. But on this day, I failed her.

I do pray she will choose to forgive me. No matter what I say or do from this point, the decision rests with her. Though I apologized several times, she can choose not to forgive me and make decisions that might forever change our relationship. I do not want our relationship to change because I love her very much, but it is an option I gave her because of my actions. I pray God's love and forgiveness will win out and we can move beyond my careless actions.

Watching her come into the world and spending these last twenty years with her has been a complete joy. I want so much to spend many more years with her, celebrating many significant milestones and events in her life. But I might be separated from those moments because I continued the cycle of offense.

The cycle of offense creates a wedge between you and everyone else, including God.[15] As I stated earlier,

---

[15] Proverbs 17:9.

hurting people hurt people. And because of the hurt you experienced, you might have hurt many others as well. If you have created a cycle of offense, there are three things you must do:

1. Repent.[16]

2. Cleanse yourself from your previous ways through God's word.[17]

3. Speak to those you offended, apologize, and ask for forgiveness.

God is greater than your heart.[18] He can help you overcome the pain and guilt from continuing a cycle of offense. God can redeem the time with your relationships and share opportunities for healing, love, and forgiveness.[19]

Reflection

How has the cycle of offense affected your life?

As a result of being offended, describe how you might have offended others.

---

[16] Acts 26:20.

[17] Psalm 119:5, 105.

[18] 1 John 3:20–21.

[19] Ephesians 5:15–16.

Pray about a time you can speak to those you offended to apologize and ask for forgiveness. Describe your conversations and whether they accepted your apology and forgiveness.

REVENGE

When many people are offended, they want revenge. They want their offender to pay for their actions. They want them to hurt, be miserable, and suffer in every way imaginable. I know I did.

Months after I learned about the offense committed against me, I wanted revenge. I wanted this person to pay for what they did to me. This was my prayer. I did not care if God struck them down or the earth swallowed them whole. I wanted justice. I wanted to be vindicated for my many years of suffering. But such desires come with a price.

Consider the parable Jesus shared about a servant that owed a significant amount of money.[20] The king brought this man before him because he had a debt of about twenty years of a laborer's wages. Because he could not repay the king, the king commanded that he, his wife and children, and all he owed be sold to settle his debt.

The servant fell down and worshipped the king. He said, "*Lord, have patience with me, and I will pay thee all.*" The king was moved with compassion, let him go, and forgave the entire debt.

---

[20] Matthew 18:21–35.

But this same servant went out and found one of his fellowservants who owed him only a day's wage. He laid his hands on him and took him by the throat. He said, "*Pay me that thou owest.*"

The fellowservant fell down at his feet, and said, "*Have patience with me, and I will pay thee all.*" But the servant would not have patience with him. He went and cast the fellowservant into prison until he could pay the debt.

When the king's fellowservants saw what the servant had done, they told the king everything he did. The king brought the servant back and said, "*O thou wicked servant, I forgave thee all that debt, because thou desiredst me: Shouldest not thou also have had compassion on thy fellowservant, even as I had pity on thee?*" The king became angry and delivered the servant to the tormentors until he could pay the original debt he owed.

So likewise shall my heavenly Father do also unto you, if ye from your hearts forgive not every one his brother their trespasses.

—Matthew 18:34–35

When you have revenge in your heart, you do not want to have anything to do with those who offended you. You do not want to see them or talk to them, let alone forgive them. You choose to intentionally hate them and seek revenge.[21] But instead of seeking revenge, consider a response of compassion and forgiveness:[22]

Put on therefore, as the elect of God, holy and beloved, bowels of mercies, kindness, humbleness of mind, meekness, longsuffering; Forbearing one another, and forgiving one another, if any man have a quarrel against any: even as Christ forgave you, so also do ye. And above all these things put on charity, which is the bond of perfectness. And let the peace of God rule in your hearts, to the which also ye are called in one body; and be ye thankful. Let the word of Christ dwell in you richly in all wisdom; teaching and admonishing one another in psalms and hymns and spiritual songs, singing with grace in your hearts to the Lord. And whatsoever ye do in word or deed, do all in the name of the Lord Jesus, giving thanks to God and the Father by him.

—Colossians 3:12–17

God loved you so much that He gave His only begotten Son, Jesus.[23] God did not wait for you to be *good*. He met you right where you were, in the midst of your sinful behavior. God could have taken

---

[21] 1 John 4:7–21.

[22] Romans 12:14–21.

[23] John 3:16.

vengeance against you in your sinful state. Yet, He showed you mercy.

As God draws you into His family, He desires you to show mercy toward others, including those who wrong you.[24] The compassion the king first showed the servant and what God showed you is founded in mercy. Mercy is founded in love. Forgiveness is love in action.

Blessed are the merciful: for they shall obtain mercy.
—Matthew 5:7

Reflection

Have you ever sought revenge for the wrongs committed against you? If so, please explain, and share the outcome.

Have you sought to extend compassion and forgiveness to those who offended you? If so, please explain, and share the outcome.

Read Matthew 18:21–35 and share your thoughts.

---

[24] Ephesians 2:18–19.

ILLUSION OF PEACE

The pain from offense can be profound and unrelenting. All you want is to heal and move on. But the more you try to move on, the tighter offense and pain grips your heart. When your reality of pain and offense does not change, or you feel you cannot escape your circumstances, you might seek an *illusion* to escape it or protect yourself from further pain.[25]

There could be one (or more) illusions you might seek to find *peace*. You might use alcohol, drugs, illicit sex (promiscuity), and other sinful vices. There are others that might take on a different persona or characteristics that are contrary to their true self. Or they could reflect characteristics of their former self (before the offense occurred) to mask their true feelings. But illusions come with their own price to pay.

As illusions fade, the hurt and pain reappear. You may return to your illusions several times to temporarily ease the pain. However, you may not realize the negative impact illusions have on your life and those around you.

---

[25] An illusion in this context is a deceptive appearance or impression.

Consider the walls you have placed around your heart and life. Think about how you have distanced yourself (physically and emotionally) from the people who love you. *What about strongholds of isolation, shame, depression, addiction, or sin that form as a result of your illusions?*

Illusions only increase your problems, they do not solve them. The aftermath from illusions can cause you to face both the pain from your offense *and* the guilt and consequences of each illusion. Your illusions become a prison where no one gets in, and you do not get out.[26]

You do not have to continue living with illusions.[27] You can have true healing, relief, and peace. These are yours to have...and always have been. Jesus has always been on your side.[28]

Reflection

Have you used *illusions of peace* in your life? If yes, please describe each illusion. How have illusions prevented you from experiencing lasting healing, relief, and peace?

If you have used illusions in the past, what were some of the consequences you experienced as a result?

_____

[26] Proverbs 18:19.

[27] Hebrews 12:1–4.

[28] Hebrews 13:5.

SECRET PLACE

He that dwelleth in the secret place of the most High shall abide under the shadow of the Almighty. I will say of the Lord, He is my refuge and my fortress: my God; in him will I trust.

—Psalm 91:1-2

As you address the offense and unforgiveness in your life, you need a place where you can pour out your heart and emotions. You need a place you can scream and yell. You need a place you can find rest and peace. You need a place where you can hear the still, small voice of the Lord. You need a secret place.

Having a secret place was an important part of my process toward forgiveness. I needed a place where I could cry and share my unfiltered thoughts and emotions with God. When I emptied myself of my anger, frustration, and rage, God filled me. He filled me with His love. God encouraged me, strengthened me, and gave me peace.

I currently have four secret places where I meet the Lord. My first secret place is being outdoors at night. I enjoy the peace and serenity that the evening brings. It gives me time to be alone and think, to hear my thoughts dance across my mind. In these moments, I feel free to pour out my soul to God. It is my special time to speak to Him and Him to me.

My second secret place is driving in my car. Whether in the day or at night, I enjoy driving on long, quiet roads. I find roads that surround me with a similar peace and serenity. I look for places I can talk aloud to God without onlookers thinking I am crazy. Sometimes I need to yell.

My third secret place is the house of the Lord. It is an amazing experience to meet God in His sanctuary. I go at times when other people are not present. I often pray, dance, read my Bible, listen to music, or sit in His presence.

When facing the 17-year offense against me, I wanted to quiet the excruciating pain in my heart. I was suffocating under the weight of my emotions. I was having a hard time seeing beyond the rage, loneliness, and depression in my soul. But on one night, instead of reaching out to one of my illusions, I went to God in my last secret place, my empty house.

Pacing back and forth in my living room, I poured out my frustrations, emotions, and heart before God. I kept repeating Psalm 147:3:

He healeth the broken in heart, and bindeth up their wounds.

After about fifteen minutes, the Lord told me I would be all right. Then I felt the binding of my wounds as if He tied them together like wood or sticks. Immediately, I felt better, and the pain subsided.

That night, I learned that God can heal my broken heart. I did not need an illusion. Illusions are temporary, but what God can provide is permanent. Only He can heal what no one can see.

If you are in pain and hurting, go to God in prayer. As a loving Father, God cares for you.[29] He wants to help you through every difficult moment and season in your life. He is always ready to listen and help you when you need it most.[30]

Trusting God with the sensitive issues of your heart can seem scary. It means you will have to be vulnerable, reliving your painful emotions and experiences. But for true healing to take place, I want to encourage you to share your hurt and pain with God. Go to your secret place and talk to Him. Share your fears and concerns. Open your heart and tell Him how you feel. Allow God to comfort you.

Now, not every thought in your mind and heart might be entirely godly...and that is all right. What you are doing in these moments is sharing your rawest thoughts and emotions. Like pouring water into a glass, you are giving God everything within you, good and bad. And as you pour yourself out before Him,

---

[29] Psalm 55:22; 1 Peter 5:7.

[30] Psalm 46:1.

He will fill you with His love. God will direct you, instruct you, and give you peace.

Come unto me, all ye that labour and are heavy laden, and I will give you rest.

—Matthew 11:28

Reflection

Do you currently have a secret place where you meet the Lord? If so, please describe each secret place and what makes it special and unique.

If you do not have a secret place, pray about locations you can go to find privacy and peace with God. After you discover one or more secret places, describe what makes each one special and unique.

TRUST

Trust in him at all times; ye people, pour out your heart before him: God is a refuge for us. Selah.
—Psalm 62:8

Because offense occurs in our lives, we sometimes lose trust in God. We expected Him to protect us and shield us from all hurt, harm, and pain. We feel let down and might not trust Him to heal and deliver us now.

Through the offense I experienced, I did not trust God to help me right away. I wondered why He allowed the offense to go for so long. So I blamed myself. Maybe there was something wrong with me, or this was punishment for something I did to someone else.

For a while, I thought I did not deserve God's deliverance. But I came to understand that experiencing hardships does not mean God does not love me or cannot deliver me.[31] He has already given me both His deliverance and love through His Son.[32]

---

[31] Isaiah 59:1; 2 Corinthians 4:7–11; 2 Timothy 3:12; James 1:1–4.

[32] John 6:44; Ephesians 2:4–5; 1 John 4:10.

God knows what I am experiencing—nothing in this world happens without His knowledge.[33] He simply has a different plan for my life than what I imagined for myself.[34]   And though I did not understand why things happened the way they did at the time, I could not allow those unknown areas to keep me from trusting Him.

I know God is good. He has blessed me and my family and been faithful in so many areas of my life. I must trust God to be just as faithful in this situation —I just do not know when or how. And even if my situation does not change, my faith and trust in God must remain.[35]

Saving the World

When Joseph was sold into slavery by his brothers and taken to Egypt, he did not allow his circumstances to dismantle his trust and faith in God. Joseph remained faithful to God when propositioned for sex by his master's wife.[36] He remained faithful after she falsely accused him of attempted rape and was sent to prison.

---

[33] Exodus 3:1–10; Psalm 139:1-18; Proverbs 15:3; Jeremiah 16:17; Matthew 10:29–30; John 1:45–51; Acts 15:18; 1 John 3:20.

[34] Isaiah 55:8–9; 1 Corinthians 6:19–20.

[35] Daniel 3:1–30.

[36] Genesis 39:1–20.

Joseph was faithful in the midst of the offenses committed against him. He maintained a good report in spite of his circumstances.[37] And after thirteen years of affliction, God delivered Joseph, making him second in charge of Egypt.[38] He would ultimately save all the world, including his brothers.[39] He would forgive them for selling him into slavery:[40]

But as for you, ye thought evil against me; but God meant it unto good, to bring to pass, as it is this day, to save much people alive.

—Genesis 50:20

God used instances of jealousy, hatred, and offense against Joseph to bring about a plan to save many people.[41] It was a plan none of them could foresee, but one orchestrated by God.

My Pain Your Glory

For my thoughts are not your thoughts, neither are your ways my ways, saith the Lord. For as the heavens are higher than the earth, so are my ways higher than

---

[37] Genesis 39:21–23.

[38] Genesis 41:1–46.

[39] Genesis 41:56–57.

[40] Genesis 45:1–7.

[41] Genesis 37:3–11.

your ways, and my thoughts than your thoughts.

—Isaiah 55:8–9

I know God saw my many years of trials and tribulation. I know He saw my broken heart. (God even confirmed it to my offender). *So why would He allow this to happen?* In response, God told me He was doing this for His glory.

My pain for Your glory?!

Many years ago, God told me that my life was a drink offering poured out to the world. He would use my life experiences as a testimony for Him. This is why I write books like *Forgive*. God uses my life as a means to help others and bring glory to Himself.

Ye are the light of the world. A city that is set on an hill cannot be hid. Neither do men light a candle, and put it under a bushel, but on a candlestick; and it giveth light unto all that are in the house. Let your light so shine before men, that they may see your good works, and glorify your Father which is in heaven.

—Matthew 5:14–16

Through your life and good works, others will be able to see the glory of God. You are His representative to share His message of love and grace in the world.[42] But sometimes, the message you share

---

[42] 2 Corinthians 5:20.

and the love and support you give comes through (and in spite of) the pain you experience. Your experiences help others to see the greatness that only exists in God.[43]

Do not allow offense and unforgiveness to dim your light in the world. God has not forgotten you. Allow Him to heal your heart and help you live in freedom. I believe He wants to give you beauty for ashes, the oil of joy for mourning, and the garment of praise for the spirit of heaviness.[44] He wants to plant (and establish) you in such a way that you will be called a tree of righteousness so that He might be glorified.

Like Joseph, may you be encouraged to place your trust in God and know He will never leave you or forsake you. Deliverance and freedom can one day be yours. Trust Him to help you see and experience life anew.

Reflection

What has been the easiest and hardest part of trusting God with your current circumstances and the direction of your life?

---

[43] 1 John 4:4.

[44] Isaiah 61:3.

If you have not trusted God with your current circumstances, are you prepared to place your complete trust in Him? Why or why not?

In what ways has God used your pain for His glory?

FORGIVENESS

The goal of forgiveness is to treat an offender as if he or she never wronged you. Within this chapter, I will address the three reasons why most people choose not to forgive: 1) pride, 2) an unwillingness to separate their emotions from the offense, and 3) disobedience to God and His Word.

Pride

Pride is a disproportionately large opinion of one's own self or importance. When a person's reputation or ego is attacked or injured, they might try to protect their persona. They do not want anyone to know they were offended or hurt emotionally. They do not want to be viewed as weak or a pushover. They refuse to give in. They do not want anyone to have any control over them. They want everyone to know they are the wrong person to mess with.[45]

The pride I was experiencing was in my desire for vindication. I wanted the person who offended me to know how much they hurt me. I wanted them to

---

[45] This might also be a reason why these individuals offend others—to protect their reputation and ego.

acknowledge this. I wanted my pain to be recognized. I wanted them to know my feelings mattered. I mattered. I am important enough to be loved and cared for. But no matter how many times I talked to them, they never acknowledged their offense to my satisfaction. The person would apologize, then intentionally hurt me a few days later. And with each offense, I was struggling to forgive. I felt like a fool for forgiving them only to have my heart stabbed and bludgeoned once more.

Pride goeth before destruction, and an haughty spirit before a fall.

—Proverbs 16:18

Pride can destroy your peace of mind, your relationships, and even your eternal standing with God. Because pride goes before destruction, you cannot see it coming. Everyone around you might see it, but you will not take heed to their warnings because of the high opinion you have of yourself. You do not want to seem weak or have anyone believe you were wrong.

Humility, on the other hand, is a humble or low opinion of your own importance or standing. Contrary to what some believe, humility is not a sign of weakness. An individual who displays humility exercises great self-control and strength. When you choose to follow God's word and show compassion and mercy, speak a kind word, and love instead of hate, you are displaying great strength:

He that is slow to anger is better than the mighty; and he that ruleth his spirit than he that taketh a city.
—Proverbs 16:32

When you have a humble or low opinion of your own importance, you are not devaluing who you are as a person. There is no weakness in forgiveness. It is actually to your glory (honor) to pass over a transgression.[46]

Put on therefore, as the elect of God, holy and beloved, bowels of mercies, kindness, humbleness of mind, meekness, longsuffering; Forbearing one another, and forgiving one another, if any man have a quarrel against any: even as Christ forgave you, so also do ye. And above all these things put on charity, which is the bond of perfectness. And let the peace of God rule in your hearts, to the which also ye are called in one body; and be ye thankful.
—Colossians 3:12–15

Emotions

An offense can stir a fireball of emotions within your heart. Anger. Hate. Rage. When your emotions are stirred, the pain in your heart consumes you. You

---

[46] Proverbs 19:11.

feel like you are drowning under a tidal wave of hurt and pain. Your emotions are so overwhelming that you feel as if you will never escape without numbing the pain or acting on how you feel.

As your emotions replay its sorrow, they burden your heart and soul.[47] They drain you of your life and strength. Some people even experience health problems, such as headaches, sleeplessness, hair loss, or weight gain or loss. Others experience anxiety, irritability, anger, depression, a lack of focus, etc.[48] Most of all, your emotions can keep you from obeying God.

With so much at stake, it is important for you to address your emotions in a healthy manner. You must take an active stance against the onslaught of your emotions. If you do nothing, your emotions can drive you into an abyss of negativity, depression, and sin.

In these moments, it is critical for you to reach out to God and your support system. You may not feel like praying or being around people when your heart is heavy, but this is when seeking God and using your support system is most needed. Sometimes having a friend in the room with you or silently listening on

---

[47] Proverbs 17:22.

[48] "Stress symptoms: Effects on your body and behavior," Mayo Clinic, accessed February 8. 2017, http://www.mayoclinic.org/healthy-lifestyle/stress-management/in-depth/stress-symptoms/art-20050987.

the phone is enough. Do not travel along the road of forgiveness alone.

Disobedience

Get your Bible and place it in your hands. In your hands is the greatest and most influential book ever written in the history of humanity. Think about what it contains: life, truth, righteousness, love, grace, etc. The Bible contains *everything* you need for life and godliness.

Because of my pride and emotions, I was not thinking about obeying God. I did not want to hear anything about showing love, peace, or forgiveness toward my offender. So I spent months being disobedient to God and His Word because I was hurt, angry, and bitter. I was not thinking about my eternal salvation or anyone else's. Who knows what could have happened to me...if it was not for God's grace.[49]

For if ye forgive men their trespasses, your heavenly Father will also forgive you: But if ye forgive not men their trespasses, neither will your Father forgive your trespasses.

—Matthew 6:14–15

Unforgiveness comes with an extremely high consequence. If you do not forgive those who

---

[49] 2 Peter 3:9.

wronged you (regardless of the offense), God will not forgive you. If your sins are not forgiven, you are not covered under the blood Jesus shed for all humanity. And without His covering, the payment for your sins is death, and eternal separation from God.[50] Unforgiveness is not a price worth paying! But the price you do owe every person is love.[51]

Master, which is the great commandment in the law? Jesus said unto him, Thou shalt love the Lord thy God with all thy heart, and with all thy soul, and with all thy mind. This is the first and great commandment. And the second is like unto it, Thou shalt love thy neighbour as thyself.

—Matthew 22:36–39

Loving others as yourself is a command, not a suggestion. It is the standard for how you should treat and interact with your neighbor. Your neighbor represents every person, not only someone you like or those who treat you kindly. Your neighbor includes those who wronged you.

Do not allow pride or your emotions to keep you from obeying God. Allow forgiveness to be your response of love and obedience.

---

[50] Romans 6:23.

[51] Romans 13:8.

Reflection

How has pride kept you from forgiving others?

Have you ever felt overwhelmed by your emotions because of an offense committed against you? If so, please explain and share the steps you have taken.

Were you ever disobedient to God and His Word because of pride or your emotions? If so, please explain, and share the outcome.

WALK IT OUT

Forgiveness is a decision.

Through God's help, I learned it did not matter if the person ever acknowledged hurting me. Forgiveness is not just something I extend to my offender, it is for me as well. Forgiveness is for my mental, physical, and spiritual health.

The discretion of a man deferreth his anger; and it is his glory to pass over a transgression.

—Proverbs 19:11

To show discretion is to use knowledge, prudence, understanding, or wisdom. In the times when I was emotional, I allowed my anger to have its way, like water bursting through a dam. I did not hold it back or defer it. However, I must be able to show discretion to push back my anger, pride, and other emotions.

I will also need to pass over the transgression committed against me. To pass over something is to not select it. This is similar to someone being passed over for a promotion or a job. I have to intentionally choose not to think about the offense committed against me. I must pass over it for something else.

Thou wilt keep him in perfect peace, whose mind is stayed on thee: because he trusteth in thee.

—Isaiah 26:3

Finally, brethren, whatsoever things are true, whatsoever things are honest, whatsoever things are just, whatsoever things are pure, whatsoever things are lovely, whatsoever things are of good report; if there be any virtue, and if there be any praise, think on these things.

—Philippians 4:8

Instead of thinking about the offense committed against me, I should keep my mind on the Lord and things that are true, honest, just, pure, lovely, and of good report, virtue, and praise. Consider the peace you will have by keeping your mind on God. Think how such thoughts would encourage you and brighten your day when your mind and heart are not consumed with anger and revenge.[52] Then your thoughts can lead to godly actions rather than actions that extend the cycle of offense or create illusions of peace.

The Decision

The day came when I decided to forgive my offender. I prayed and came to a better understanding

---

[52] Proverbs 17:22.

of the hurt and pain I caused them so many years earlier, as well as the pain and offense stemming from their childhood. I wanted them to find true healing and peace through God. I wanted them to be made whole:

Heavenly Father, I ask that you would forgive my offender. I pray that you would help them heal and find peace. Restore our relationship and allow our lives to be made anew. Help us grow beyond our once painful circumstances. If there is any unforgiveness or offense in them, please assist them in finding healing, love, and forgiveness. May they experience the same freedom you have graciously given me. In the name of Jesus Christ, I pray, Amen.

This was how I knew I reached a *place* of forgiveness. I no longer carried the same anger or hatred. Nor were my words hollow representations of the truth. From my heart, I meant every word. And I treated them in the exact manner I had before the offense occurred.

Reattacks

Now, there may come a time when my mind or heart wants to take a few steps backward. This might happen if the *offender* returns to their previous offensive words and actions. This is typically when my pride or emotions want to rise up and flood my mind and heart. But I cannot allow them to roam free in my mind.[53]

If I give into these thoughts, they will drag me back into the abyss of anger, pride, and unforgiveness. So I must acknowledge and submit to God's sovereignty over my life.[54]　I must go into my secret place to pray. I can also review scriptures that address the matter at hand and the steps God gave me for showing compassion and mercy. This is my process for resisting the devil and any evil thoughts coming against me.

As I work through this *process*, the thoughts will begin to subside. But I have to stay with it. I must continue to maintain my position of obedience, love, and forgiveness.

70 X 7

Then came Peter to him, and said, Lord, how oft shall my brother sin against me, and I forgive him? till seven times? Jesus saith unto him, I say not unto thee, Until seven times: but, Until seventy times seven.

—Matthew 18:21–22

Each time someone sins against me, I cannot keep a record of their wrongdoing. Whether they ask for forgiveness or not, I have to forgive them. I have to

---

[53] 2 Corinthians 10:3–5.

[54] James 4:7.

treat them as if they never wronged me. And I cannot try to establish *protective measures* for fear of being offended and hurt again.

If I use protective measures, such as adjusting how I speak or act around the offender, I am keeping a record of wrongs. My protective measures would be based on the original offense. I would not be walking in true forgiveness.

How do you think a person can be wronged 490 times? They forgive the offender from the heart after each instance. They return to the exact mental, emotional, and physical state before the offense occurred. This becomes a deliberate decision they make through love and obedience, not through pride or emotions.

Reflection

Please take a moment to read Matthew 5 and 1 Corinthians 13:1–8. How you can apply these scriptures toward a response of forgiveness?

(com)mission™
PUBLISHING

www.commissionpubs.com
info@commissionpubs.com

www.ingramcontent.com/pod-product-compliance
Lightning Source LLC
Chambersburg PA
CBHW071646040426
42452CB00009B/1785